T0149419

EFFECTIVE BELIEFS

Towards Individual
and Group Harmony;
a Challenge to People
of Goodwill

NOEL W. DAVIS

BALBOA.
PRESS

A DIVISION OF HAY HOUSE

Balboa Press books may be ordered through booksellers or by contacting:

Balboa Press
A Division of Hay House
1663 Liberty Drive
Bloomington, IN 47403
www.balboapress.com.au
1 (877) 407-4847

Print information available on the last page.

ISBN: 978-1-5043-1447-3 (sc)
ISBN: 978-1-5043-1448-0 (e)

Balboa Press rev. date: 08/31/2018

This book is dedicated to my family, Mary, Paul, Stephen and Mark. Also the various pets – world harmony in microcosm perhaps.

PREFACE

There was a time when, having been steeped in the Christian tradition I thought that for the world to be a better place the peoples of the world needed to become Christian. At that point when people had the same or similar beliefs there would be a basis for understanding. I have long since come to believe that such a course is an impossibility. For a start one would have to ask what brand of Christianity is being considered.

This book is written out of the conviction that a person's beliefs have a direct bearing on their attitudes and actions and that beliefs can be modified so that they result in effective, positive outcomes.

There is no attempt to make this an academic exercise. It is a coming together of thoughts which have been developing for many years. The book is designed to be a guide to positively effective living with an avoidance of gobbledegook of any description.

The book is aimed towards people of goodwill whether they are Hindus, Jews, Buddhists, Christians, Muslims, Humanists, Atheists, Agnostics or those who espouse no particular belief.

THE PREAMBLE

This book is based on four principles:–

1. What a person believes governs their attitudes and actions.
2. That unless someone is in some way severely mentally impaired, they have beliefs.
3. The effectiveness of beliefs is ultimately shown by their outcomes.
4. That to endeavour to convince others to align themselves to one's particular beliefs blocks efforts at co-operation.

-ooOoo-

1. Examples bearing out this principle are almost numberless, three will suffice. If one believes that a particular race is supreme then there will be no concern for how those who are not of that race are treated.

    If one believes that they have no responsibility for the state of the environment they will make no effort to conserve it.

1

If one believes that differences can be reconciled through dialogue in spite of mammoth differences in view point there can be reconciliation. The power of belief cannot be overestimated. This is well born out with the Placebo effect. The word comes from a Latin root meaning, "I shall be pleasing or acceptable".

Time and again it has been shown that when treatment is suggested for a particular ailment, if one group of people is given an actual form of medication with the others receiving a form which looks the same but could be a sugar pill, the positive outcomes in the control group are very high because the participants believe they are receiving something beneficial.

In his fascinating book "Timeless Healing", Herbert Benson MD sets out his work on this effect. He suggests a different name for the phenomenon to remove the negative connotations which are sometimes associated with it, making it a form of "hocus pocus". The term he uses is "remembered wellness".

He lists three components: "1. Belief and expectancy on behalf of the patient; 2. Belief and expectancy on behalf of the caregiver; and 3. Belief and expectancies generated by the relationship between the patient and the caregiver"[1]. He makes

---

[1]   "Timeless Healing", Herbert Benson MD, p. 32.

the statement "In every incident of remembered wellness, the catalyst is belief . . . As humans we are laden with beliefs, influences so interwoven we cannot precisely distinguish their sources"[2]. It is my contention that the effectiveness of belief in regard to health issues also applies to belief in general.

2. The beliefs of a great number of people on planet earth are very obvious because of their allegiance to one of the ancient and well established belief systems such as Hinduism, Judaism, Buddhism, Christianity and Islam. In spite of the time honoured nature of these beliefs, it is my contention that there is no exclusive meaning system which leads to the outcomes in the checklist to come.

There will be no attempt to find similarities between the priorities or doctrines of the various religions. For the purposes of this book religion is given its broadest possible definition as a "Search for Meaning". Certainly it is true that a number of people could be surprised that that they have beliefs in that they may not have formalised them but there are four questions which in your thoughtful moments you may have sought to answer consciously or unconsciously: "Who am I?"; "What am I?"; "How can I make sense of the existence in which I find myself?"; and "How can I handle this existence?"

---

2   "Timeless Healing", Herbert Benson MD, p. 38.

The German word "weltanshaung", usually translated, "world view" suggests a broad approach to beliefs in general. In his book "Man's Search for Meaning", Victor Frankl wrote "Any attempt to restore a man's inner strength had first to succeed in showing him some future goal."[3]

I recognise that followers of established belief systems may find it off putting to be cast in the same light as those whose beliefs may not have been formalised. By the same token those who have spent a large section of their lives trying to make plain that they don't subscribe to any particular belief may be equally disturbed. However to say that one has no beliefs is at that point to state a belief.

3.   The validity and/or effectiveness of beliefs is shown by their outcomes. This principle is at the heart of the argument of this book. It is not enough when the wellbeing of the individual and society is being considered to maintain beliefs on the basis of their long tradition or because they happen to be enshrined in what is regarded as some sacred text. I'm not saying that beliefs which are held on this basis are necessarily not positively effective, just that the ultimate test of the validity of beliefs is their positive outcomes.

Jesus is recorded as saying about people bringing a message "Beware of false prophets! You can tell

---

[3]   p.121

what they are by what they do. No one picks grapes or figs from thorn bushes."[4]

This is the basis for the checklist which constitutes the greatest part of this book. It is made up of the 10 outcomes which I consider to be crucial to finding individual and group harmony. They have been arrived at through a lifetime of reading, study, thought and association with people of different cultures, races and to some extent beliefs. As indicated in the Preface I happen to have grown up in a Christian home of the Methodist variety and have been trained in the Methodist ministry. I gladly joined the Uniting Church at its inception. Over the years, however, I have moved to the left of the theological spectrum and call myself a Christian Humanist. I feel that the items on the checklist can be arrived at through a broad spectrum of beliefs.

My studies have been mostly in the fields of the Bible, Christian Theology, Philosophy, Psychology, Education and Pastoral Care. A particular learning experience has been an association with those whose critical acuity cannot be questioned, High School students, in my time as a School Chaplain.

It is my hope that those reading this book will recognise the value of the attitudes in the checklist and, if necessary, modify their beliefs so that positive outcomes are possible. In his book "Fully

---

[4] "Man's Search for Meaning", Victor Frankl.

Human, Fully Alive", John Powell gives hope of this happening with his words, "My attitude has changed therefore everything has changed."

4. There is no attempt at proselytisation as to do so immediately suggests the superiority of a particular belief. The way towards group harmony will be through open dialogue between people of different beliefs each sharing what they believe and being open to hearing the beliefs of others. In a book published in 1963 Reuel L Howe spoke of the place of dialogue in the community. I don't think the sentiment expressed in the title is excessive, "The Miracle of Dialogue". He wrote "When dialogue stops, love dies and resentment and hatred are born."[5] Some of the requirements of dialogue are well set out by John Bodycomb in his book "No Fixed Address" in his recollection of a conversation with Krister Stendahl, Dean of Harvard Divinity School. "First principle was that if I wanted to know something about another faith, I should ask some knowledgeable active member to tell me about it. Second principle was 'compare like with like', it is quite improper to compare our best with their worst. The third principle is, 'learn how to cultivate a 'holy envy'. Learn to see something beautiful in the other's faith that is not yours but that you wish was yours."[6]

---

[5]   Miracle of Dialogue. Reuel L. Howe. p. 3

[6]   "No Fixed Address", John Bodycomb, p. 141 – p. 142.

It is encouraging that there are a number of signs that there is an increasing degree of openness between many beliefs throughout the world. Hans Kung in his book "A Global Ethic" has made the comment "There can be no peace among the nations without peace among the religions"[7]. "A Global Ethic" is "The Declaration of the Parliament of the World's Religions". At the parliament of 1993 there were some 70 different religions present. Succeeding parliaments have had even greater representation. Such gatherings give definite hope of greater group, even world harmony.

Another movement which is gathering momentum is "The Charter for Compassion". It came about through the following wish of Karen Armstrong, the writer of a number of exhaustively researched books on religious topics such as "Battle for God"; "I wish that you would help with the creation, launch and propagation of a Charter for Compassion, charted by a group of leading inspirational thinkers from the three Abrahamic traditions of Judaism, Christianity and Islam and based on the fundamental principles of universal justice and respect."

Her wish sparked off a movement which has drawn up a charter. The writing of the charter was open to people all around the world of all faith traditions and backgrounds. The online writing took place in the Fall of 2008. In February of 2009

---

[7] "A Global Ethic", Hans Kung, Karl-Josef Kushel, p. 4.

the contributions were collected and given to the Council of Conscience. The Council is a multi-faith, multi-national group of religious thinkers and leaders. They reviewed and sorted the contributions to craft the final chapter. People from 100 countries added their views and the charter has been translated into more than 30 languages. One of its clauses reads "We therefore call upon all men and women, to restore compassion to the centre of morality and religion – to return to the ancient principle that any interpretation of scripture that breeds violence, hatred or disdain is illegitimate".

Another indication of the existing climate towards understanding between beliefs is found in a little book by Kwok Pui-Lan, "Globalisation, Gender and Peacebuilding – The Future of Interfaith Dialogue". She uses the term "polydoxy", which is as fascinating a term to me as "orthodoxy" which has been used for centuries to indicate established traditional beliefs. She defines the term as follows "Polydoxy, as its prefix 'poly' suggests acknowledges both the internal diversity of the Christian tradition and the plurality of the world's religious and spiritual traditions. Coleen Hartung has said "Polydoxy, a space for many opinions about beliefs within a body of beliefs, or alternatively a place of many faiths within a circle of faith, implies an openness to diversity, difference, challenge and multiplicity."[8]

---

[8] "Globalisation, Gender and Peacebuilding – The Future of Interfaith Dialogue", Kwok Pui-Lan, p. 69.

Indicating the interest in a middle of the road approach to mutual understanding and harmony is a book by M. Scott Peck published in 1993 "A World Waiting to be Born". In it he puts forward the place of civility in society. He writes, "I wish to resurrect and redefine the meaning of civility. This is necessary for the healing of our society."[9]

He moves towards defining civility in the following statement, "Civility certainly does have to do with how we humans relate with each other. Whenever there is a relationship between two or more people, an organisation of some sort is involved. Genuine civility is then, in part, consciously motivated organisational behaviour."[10] It seems a very low key idea but towards the end of the book he mentions the formation of a "Foundation for Community Encouragement". As I had never heard of such an organisation in Australia I doubted if the idea had ever taken off. On googling the name of the organisation I found that it had flourished. It indicates the presence in society of a grassroots, maybe a largely silent majority of people who see the need to get beyond differences of culture, race and belief.

---

[9] "A World Waiting to be Born – Civility Rediscovered", M. Scott Peck, p. 4.

[10] "A World Waiting to be Born – Civility Rediscovered", M. Scott peck, p. 5.

I came across a more recent corroboration of the presence in society of a middle of the road approach in an interview with Hugh Mackay, Social Researcher, who referred to himself as a 'Christian agnostic".

He had been speaking a great deal about "the good life" and suggests that "the good life is about our commitment to the so-called Golden Rule, treat others the way you would like to be treated."[11]

This particular section defines what I mean in the title when directing a "challenge to people of goodwill." While I welcome warmly the movement toward greater understanding between people of different beliefs, the thrust of this book is to ask what positive effects the various beliefs have and to suggest ten areas in which people's responses can have a definite bearing on individual and group harmony.

We have been, perforce, speaking about various belief or interest groups but if we're thinking change and maximising effect, the starting point is very individual. John Honeywill, an artist coming to greater prominence, suggests that one needs to act locally while thinking globally and quotes "All good art is local and that's what makes it universal". There is a very apt story which narrows the focus still further.

---

[11]   Week end Australian, 7-8 September 2013, Hugh Mackay, p. 8.

"A wise, old middle-eastern mystic said this about himself. I was a revolutionary when I was young and all my prayer to God was: Lord, give me the energy to change the world. As I approached middle age and realised that my life was half gone without my changing a single soul, I changed my prayer to: Lord give me the grace to change all those who come into contact with me. Just my family and friends and I shall be satisfied. Now that I am an old man and my days are numbered, I have begun to see how foolish I have been. My one prayer now is: Lord, give me the grace to change myself. If I had prayed for this right from the start, I would not have wasted my life."[12]

[12]   "Stories and Parables for Preachers and Teachers, Paul Wharton, p. 31.

THE CHECKLIST

The ten attitudes which follow are those which I consider are essential to be espoused for individual and/or group harmony. The challenge is to see if your beliefs include or lead to these attitudes. If they don't, I respectfully suggest your beliefs are found wanting.

NOTE - THE FIRST TWO ATTITUDES MUST BE IN BALANCE

Attitude 1: Getting Oneself in Perspective

For there to be individual and group harmony it is essential that the beliefs of each individual enable them to recognise that they are not at the centre of the universe and that the world doesn't revolve around them. A human infant is the most dependent offspring of any member of the animal kingdom and for the longest.

As a matter of survival a human infant has to be demanding and the centre of attention. It is tragic if any individual is not cared for and helped to get beyond demanding attention or has excessive attention lavished on them. As more mature individuals our beliefs need to encourage the displacement of egocentrism otherwise there is no concern for the wellbeing and harmony of the rest of the world. It is strange but true that displacing oneself from the centre of existence has a direct bearing on one's individual sense of wellbeing.

Donald Cupitt, sometimes called "the atheist priest", speaks of "solar ethics". In other words an attitude to life which like the sun exists to give of itself. He wrote, "I say flatly that there is no inner space within the self through which we have access to another world more real than this one, and indeed there simply isn't any other world than this one, the common public world that is generated by our expressions and our symbolic exchanges. We do, we must, come out to live."[13]

In his intriguing book "A Religion for Atheists" Alain de Botton wrote, "Science should matter to us not only because it helps us to control parts of the world, but also because it shows us things that we will never master. Thus we do well to meditate daily, rather as the religious do on their God, on the 9.5 trillion kilometres which comprise a single light year, or perhaps the luminosity of the largest known star in our galaxy, Eta Carinae, 7,500 light years distant, 400 times the size of the sun and 4 million times as bright.

We should punctuate our calendars with celebrations in honour of VY Canis Majoris, a red hyper giant in the constellation of Canis Major 5000 light years from earth and 2,100 times bigger than our sun. Nightly, perhaps after the main news bulletin and before the celebrity quiz, we might observe a moment of silence in order to contemplate the 200 to 400 billion stars in our galaxy, the 100 billion galaxies and the 3 septillion stars in the universe. Whatever their value may be to science, the stars are in the end no less

---

[13]   "Solar Ethics", Donald Cupitt p.9

valuable to mankind as solutions to our megalomania, self-pity and anxiety." [14]

BUT

Attitude 2: Each Individual has a Vital and Unique Place

There is not one individual who is the complete replica of any other in the total world population. There is not one individual who should ever be regarded as expendable for the whims or purposes of any other. Apart from anything else, if one desires, we exist to pass on our unique genes. Our beliefs need to encourage a sense of self-esteem so that one recognises one's own uniqueness and the contribution which she/he alone can make to the greater wellbeing of humankind and all living things on earth.

I have trouble singing the words of the first verse of the amazingly popular hymn, "Amazing grace, how sweet the sound that saved a wretch like me." I don't see myself as a wretch although I understand where John Newton, the author, was coming from as he had been the captain of a ship involved in the horrendous slave trade. To put oneself in perspective does not necessitate seeing oneself as being of little worth.

In his helpful book, "I'm OK, You're OK" Thomas Harris makes Freudian psychology much more accessible. He suggests that to have a worthwhile approach to life one needs to keep in balance the sense that one is her/himself okay while not allowing that sense to prevent the acceptance

---

[14] "Religion for Atheists", Alain de Botton p.202

of okay-ness in others. It is this balance that I am putting forward in the first two items of the checklist.

There is further backing in a letter Paul, the apostle, wrote to the church in Rome "For I say through the grace given unto me, to every person that is among you, not to think of himself more highly than he ought to think." In other words he's suggesting that it is okay to think well of oneself but not to overdo it. I have to say that Paul, on occasions, in his letters revealed that he had a rather healthy ego.

NOTE – ATTITUDES 3 & 4 NEED TO BE CONSIDERED TOGETHER

Attitude 3: A Sense of Community

The best of our humanness is not available without a sense of community. There have been people who have survived for long periods in solitary confinement but usually this has been, at least partially possible through memory of community and/or in anticipation of a return to community.

A community provides us with possibilities of companionship, support, example, guidance. The basic unit is the family which, when functioning well, helps us to experience living with others and to value interdependence. Since most of us have neither the experience nor the time to handle all the tasks necessary to live from day to day, being in a community means dependence on the varying skills and interests of other members.

So, for example, the growth and transportation of food, the construction of houses, roads and other forms of infrastructure are provided by members of the community.

A sense of community is possible because of the following fact pointed out by Rev. Susan Sparks in her intriguing book "Laugh your way to Grace." We will be making larger use of the book later in the checklist.

"Scientists in mapping the human gene have determined that human beings are in fact 99.9% genetically the same. Religion, skin colour, ethnicity, national origin, gender - none of these matter. We are 99.9% the same. Which means that our judgments of each other - our injustice, our violence, our warfare - are all over this 0.1% difference."[15] So our beliefs, if they are to be worthwhile need to lead to a workable sense of community.

Sadly, as indicated by the above quote from Susan Spark's book, in spite of our underlying sameness this is very often not the case. This leads us to the next item in the checklist which starts with a big

BUT

Attitude 4: A Minimising of Tribalism

It seems almost an integral part of being human is to adopt a "them" and "us" mind set. Tribalism has many forms. A tribe is a group of possibly related people living in the same area but a sense of tribalism can come about in relation to a state, nation, culture, religion or sect. Within a religion it seems endless. The impact on community is glaringly obvious. The heading says it all. I'm not sure it's possible to completely do without tribalism as we seem to need a sense of belonging but it's imperative to minimise it.

---

[15]   "Laugh your way to Grace", Rev. Susan Sparks, p. 15.

Buckminster Fuller spoke of being a "citizen of the world". Erik Erikson referred to tribes as the "pseudo-species". Both of these views suggest that it is of benefit to all to transcend tribalism as much as possible. In other words, to extend our sense of community. Point 4 of the "Preamble" speaks of the place of dialogue. Minimising tribalism demands that wherever possible we are willing to meet people who we may regard as different.

Attitude 5: Tolerance, Openness and Forgiveness

Do I hear a chorus of "pie in the sky" or "get real"? It seems, at times, to go with the territory that when we espouse beliefs, and we do all have them, we may become enthusiastic about them to the extent of finding it difficult to tolerate any other. The capacity for tolerance is a part of human nature. It just needs to be recognised and activated. There seems little chance for group harmony without acceptance of people and the beliefs they find meaningful.

Openness comes about from freedom of association. Being with other people of different backgrounds, race, colour, culture gives the possibility of the realisation that differences are indeed skin deep. It is hard to conceive of any possibility of group and world harmony if revenge is an accepted part of our beliefs. There is a saying "an eye for an eye will make the whole world blind"[15] Even those who at least with the top of their heads embrace forgiveness may find it hard to exert in practice. Hopefully those who enjoy watching movies based on violence or revenge may in this way expunge the desire to exert revenge in real life.

There is no doubt that achieving forgiveness and waiving a desire for revenge promotes a sense of individual harmony. If one seeks revenge for some hurt the effects of the hurt are extended.

Attitude 6: An Overall Espousal of Non-Violence and a Spurning of Gratuitous Violence

To espouse non-violence is to avoid open conflict and the possibility of escalation. There have been a succession of people throughout history who have adopted this position, including Jesus, Mahatma Gandhi, and Martin Luther King. This is not a position of weakness as was well illustrated by Gandhi who called his approach "satyagraha" (soul force). It is more than passive resistance, which often comes about from a feeling of weakness. There is rather a feeling of strength, a feeling that one will win through in spite of hardships."[16] A person who practices a non-violent approach removes threat and fear from relations with others.

The second part of the title of this section implies that sadly violence may, at times, not be avoidable when a person, community or nation is under threat there is a need for defence. This, of course, has been hugely debated over the years. The use of the term "gratuitous violence", in the title, indicates that I don't consider pacifism a valid option.

If one's beliefs are going to be effective in bringing about individual and group harmony the stance suggested here is absolutely essential.

---

[16] "Me, You and Others" (2), Elizabeth Callister, Noel Davis, Barbara Pope, p. 119.

As Gandhi's espousal of non-violence as "satyagraha" suggests an attitude of non-violence doesn't have to involve fearful submission. The human relationships education teaching about assertiveness is of value in this regard. If one puts aggression at one end of a scale and submissiveness at the other, assertiveness would fall in the middle.

The following description of assertive people from "Me, You and Others" defines assertiveness.

1. They stand up for themselves.
2. They are polite but firm.
3. They have respect for themselves and others.
4. They try to control their feelings and act rationally.
5. They see choices and shades of grey; they don't look at the world in narrow, black and white way.
6. They face up to situations and work at solving problems.
7. Generally, they have good eye contact, stand comfortably but firmly, and talk in a strong, steady tone of voice.
8. Assertive people don't blame other people for what they feel. They face up to their own feelings. They learn that they make themselves happy and, at times, sad or angry.
9. They use phrases like "I feel", "I think", and "I would like".
10. They are cooperative people who include and consult others, so they also use phrases like, "How can we solve this?" or "Let's try this."[17]

---

[17] "Me, You and Others", Elizabeth Callister, Noel Davis, Barbara Pope

Attitude 7: A Sense of Humour

Human beings are unique amongst the species in having the capacity to laugh. I doubt if one can find inward harmony or if there can be group, even world harmony unless this capacity is allowed to develop. People vary in their readiness to laugh and the strength of their sense of humour, but our beliefs are not being effective if they don't allow or even actively encourage laughter. Susan Sparks in her book "Laughing your way to Grace" made the following comment, "Laughter heals. It grounds us in a place of hope. Perhaps most important, laughter fosters intimacy and honesty in our relationships with each other."[18]

She further states "Like a good roll of duct tape, humour bonds us to each other. It strengthens us as a community, and it allows us to transcend our differences and our barriers. When we laugh with someone - whether it is a stranger, a friend, a lover, or an enemy - our worlds overlap for a tiny but significant moment. It is then that our defences have lowered, ideas and feelings are shared, and the best in each gleams forth."[19]

Of prime importance is the willingness to laugh at oneself when tempted to be too aware of our position or station and possibly burdened with pomposity. To share a situation which is seen to have a funny side and to laugh together about it definitely promotes harmony. Of negative effect is, of course, the cruel reaction of laughing at another's misfortunes.

---

[18] 18-29 "Laugh your way to Grace", Susan Sparks. p. 18
[19] "Laugh your way to Grace", Susan Sparks. p. 68

It is impossible to have a sense of humour without an optimistic or hopeful approach to life, unless that humour is particularly dark. Certainly there can be no individual harmony with a largely pessimistic attitude and this transfers to group harmony. A person who always sees a glass as half empty rather than half full will lack the resilience needed to seek the wellbeing of self, the community and the world.

In his book "Learned Optimism" Martin Seligman outlines compelling ways to be more optimistic and therefore positive about oneself and the world.

There is no clearer example of how a sense of humour can impact on our lives than a section of Susan Spark's book which shows how laughter helped her work through the stages of grief put forward by the psychiatrist, Elizabeth Kubler-Ross. The need for such a process came about as she wrestled with the diagnosis and treatment of cancer. My aim in this next section is to summarise her presentation using relevant quotes.

"For several weeks, denial, the first stage of grief, was my forte."[20] She lists some of the comments of people when learning she had been diagnosed with cancer, some of them rather insensitive. "The only alternative? Soften the blow through humour."[21] She did a google search on cancer and humour and found a number of sites dedicated to funny cancer products. She acquired a magnet for her refrigerator which read "Cancer - it's not just an astrological sign anymore."[22]

---

[20] "Laugh your way to Grace", Susan Sparks. p. 91
[21] "Laugh your way to Grace", Susan Sparks. p. 91
[22] "Laugh your way to Grace", Susan Sparks. p. 92

Other research showed that laughter is next to chocolate and chilli peppers as a producer of endorphins, "nature's own happy pill". "Medical studies have even shown that laughter produces the same level of mood altering endorphins as a good work out."[23]

She continues "The second stage, anger, was a bit easier for me but harder on the world."[24] She lists a number of extensive scans. One of these was a liver scan. She informed the technician that she had consumed a couple of beers the previous night. To which he replied with a sigh. He went away and came back with a grave look on his face saying that they weren't supposed to give test results on the spot, "but you clearly have the early stages of what appears to be "Bud Light" syndrome." He then burst out laughing. She finally joined him in his laughter and wrote "And while I was still mad, the laughter slowly began to chip away at my prickly fortress of anger."[25]

She then writes about dealing with the third stage which is bargaining. "After the anger started to wane, I started to whine, Why me? Why this? Why now?"[26] She started to look for alternative treatments. Her partner decided to throw a party which seemed at first grossly inappropriate. Then she found herself concerned with party arrangements rather than other possible treatments. "Much of life's stress comes from a feeling of loss of control. Choosing laughter

---

[23]   "Laugh your way to Grace", Susan Sparks.

[24]   "Laugh your way to Grace", Susan Sparks.

[25]   "Laugh your way to Grace", Susan Sparks.

[26]   "Laugh your way to Grace", Susan Sparks.

and joy over worry helps us to feel as if we have retaken control."[27]

She is the minister of a Baptist church in New York as well as having trained in law and being a stand-up comedian. As she writes of dealing with the fourth stage, depression, she recounts how members of her congregation, some with a rather quirky sense of humour helped her through. Some of them sent cards. The following from one of her senior and more proper members "I am thinking of you and hoping that you might enjoy a smile over the following quote: Eleanor Roosevelt once said, "I had a rose named after me and I was very flattered. But I was not pleased to read the inscription in the catalogue: No good in bed, but fine against a wall."" Susan Sparks wrote "I felt almost immediately better, partly because my congregation had such an irreverent sense of humour, but also because the cards and jokes offered me a sense of solidarity."[28]

Finally she writes about the last of Kubler-Ross's stages, acceptance and makes a very important point. "For me, the stages of grief were never predictable. One would never move seamlessly into another. One moment I would be in denial, then bargaining, then angry, then back to denial, then depressed; then I'd repeat the steps all over again." [29]

She writes that she knew she had reached a measure of acceptance when she and her partner went on a motorcycle trip from Jackson-Hole, Wyoming. She had just finished her last radiation treatment. As they were leaving Jackson together on the bike they stopped for a photo with the

---

[27]   "Laugh your way to Grace", Susan Sparks. p. 95
[28]   "Laugh your way to Grace", Susan Sparks. p. 96
[29]   "Laugh your way to Grace", Susan Sparks. p. 97

Grand Teton range in the background. Anyone who has passed through that part of the US would agree that it is a spectacular scene. She looked at her partner and said "There is our Christmas card … this photo with the greeting: Cancer can kiss our Tetons."[30]

She obviously came through her bout of cancer. I'm not suggesting that this extensive use of humour and laughter in dealing with being afflicted with something as threatening as cancer will work for everyone. I've used this extensive reference to Susan Spark's book to show how laughter contributes positively to worthwhile living. Our beliefs need to allow and encourage this natural part of being human.

Attitude 8: A Recognition of the Equality of the Sexes

Approximately half the world's population are women. However, through much of history, women have been often discriminated against and many times oppressed. Yet it is a fact that when women have access to education and are treated equally the quality of any society improves. There is often a reluctance in patriarchal societies to give girls/women ready access to education thus having more chance of challenging male domination. This reluctance was highlighted in October 2012 in Pakistan when Mallala Yousafzai was shot in the head in a bus. She had been a visible advocate for girl's education, campaigning for increased government spending on schools and encouraging families to break with family tradition and allow their daughters to attend classes.

---

[30] "Laugh your way to Grace", Susan Sparks. p. 97

Professor Shirley Randell, Managing Director, SRIA Rwanda Ltd. commented in a newsletter of 15 October 2012 "The greatest risk to violent extremists in Pakistan is not American drones it is educated girls." In the same newsletter she quotes a 19 year old female student "This is not just Mallala's war, it is a war between two ideologies, between the light of education and darkness."

The importance of ready access to education for girls and women was also highlighted by UNESCO when on 26 May 2011 it launched its "Global partnership for Girls and Women's Education". "Globally, some 39 million girls of lower secondary age are currently not enrolled in primary or secondary education, while two thirds of the world's 796 million illiterate adults are women." In the same release the Prime Minister of Bangladesh, Sheik Hasina, pointed out that "If you educate one boy, you educate one boy, whereas if you educate a girl, you educate her entire family and community."

The importance of tapping the resources made up of 50% of the world's population who are women has been underlined by Warren Buffet in an article for Fortune. This was quoted by Jessica Irvine in the Courier Mail of 8 May 2013 "Unleashing the talents of women offers the best hope for a new wave of productivity in the US. We've seen what can be accomplished when we use 50% of our human capacity. If you visualise what 100% can do, you'll join me as an unbridled optimist about America's future." Of course, what he said applies throughout the world.

There is another major point when we are considering group harmony. There are obvious physical differences between females and males. These differences also extend, in general, to approaches to life and in attitudes.

In their generally amusing but perceptive book "Why Men don't listen and Women Can't Read Maps", Allan and Barbara Pease highlight these differences. Certainly one needs to avoid stereotyping, but basically they are suggesting that different functions for males and females in ages past have influenced their genetic inheritance. "Spatial ability is not strong in women and girls because being able to chase animals and find their way home was never part of woman's job description."[31]

They comment in the conclusion of the book "Relationships between men and women work despite overwhelming sex differences. Much of the credit here goes to women because they have the necessary skills to manage relationships and family. They are equipped with the ability to sense the motives and meanings behind speech and behaviour, and can therefore predict outcomes or take action early to avert problems. This factor alone would make the world a much safer place if every nation's leader was a woman."[32]

The general propensity for women to co-operate and work with others is illustrated in the answer given by Jody Williams, Nobel Prize winner and activist to a question in a Time interview "How are female activists different from male activists? Shirin Abadi, who received the peace prize in 2003, said there are seven women alive who have

---

[31] "Why Men Don't Listen and Women Don't Read Maps", Allan and Barbara Pease, p. 116.

[32] "Why Men Don't Listen and Women Don't Read Maps", Allan and Barbara Pease, p.116

received the Peace Prize; shouldn't we try to think about a project we can do together? And the Nobel Women's Initiative was born. Male Peace Prize winners have never come together to use their access and influence to support building sustainable peace. Get a critical mass of women and it was the first thing we thought of."[33]

That there is a way to go before equal opportunity is achieved in some areas is shown in her answer to the question "Didn't you want to be the Pope when you were little? I applied. However, I'm married. I'm divorced. I'm heathenish. And I'm a girl. Bad combo."[33]

It is encouraging to be made aware in the media from time to time of more and more women moving into prominent positions in government, education, business and industry. There is, however, a long way to go before equality is achieved.

All the foregoing underlines the fact that if one's beliefs do not include the equality of the sexes so that each person may make a contribution to the wellbeing of society, then those beliefs are seriously lacking.

Attitude 9: Accepting Varying Sexual Preferences

When I first considered this part of the checklist I mostly had in mind acceptance of those with a homosexual preference. Then I read the words of Hon. Michael Kirby ACCMG in his foreword to "Being Gay, Being Christian You Can be Both." By Dr Stuart Edser "I hope that this book will gain a large readership among people of diverse sexualities: heterosexual, homosexual, bisexual, transgender

---

[33] Time Magazine, 25 March 2013, p. 48.

and intersexual." In other words there is a large variety in sexual preference.

So why is this topic included in a checklist to see if one's beliefs really measure up as a possible contribution to individual and group harmony? No matter how self-satisfied one may feel in their approach to life, if they have excluded from attention any group in society whose sexual preference is different from their own, then I believe their beliefs are found wanting. I want to include a rather lengthy quote from Stuart Edser's book at this stage as it establishes the basis for this section.

"Gay and lesbian people are physically and emotionally attracted to people of their own sex with whom they can form loving and sexual relationships. Just like their straight counterparts, gay and lesbian individuals come in all shapes and sizes.

We are Caucasian and Asian, black, white, tall, short, rich, poor, educated, uneducated, intelligent and not so intelligent. Some of us are people of faith and others are not. We are people with mothers, fathers, brothers, sisters, partners and children. We are introverted, extroverted, sensitive, insensitive, confident, unsure, garrulous and shy. We work as professionals, in blue collar jobs and as tradespeople. Some of us are studying. We have strengths and weaknesses, dreams and regrets, likes and dislikes and successes and failures in life. We have mortgages and personal loans, invest in the stock market and property and pay our taxes. We go to the beach, the movies, the ski fields, the pub, the café, the shopping centre and the sporting fixture … In short, gay and lesbian individuals are people, with all the variety, richness and dignity that human beings possess. Gay and lesbian people are not a behaviour.

As much as being gay is not a behaviour, neither is it some trendy thing that you decide to become. Being gay is not about parties or sex any more than being straight is. Neither should it be about denying who you are …"[34]

"The really important point made is that homosexuality is not a behaviour, neither is it some trendy thing that you decide to become. People do not decide to become homosexual or adopt any of the sexual preferences mentioned by Hon. Michael Kirby. Sexual preference is determined, genetically or biologically. Recent reputable studies have been published in which the proportion of men endorsing exclusive homosexuality ranges from 0.9% to 2% and women between 0.2% and 1%."[35]

As at the time of writing this book there is huge debate around the world to do with the recognition of homosexual and lesbian people. There has been incredible lack of understanding, judgmentalism and in some cases persecution. However, in some societies, homosexual people have been admitted to the armed services and homosexual relationships recognised. I believe this trend should continue.

For the sake of individual harmony, whatever a person's sexual preference, there needs to be an assurance of acceptance by society.

It is my firm understanding that if one's beliefs do not allow the acceptance of people of varying sexual preference then those beliefs need revision.

---

[34] "Being Gay, Being Christian", Dr Stuart Edser, p. 41 – p. 42.
[35] "Being Gay, Being Christian", Dr Stuart Edser, p. 41 – p. 42.

Attitude 10: Reverence for Life (Deep Respect for all Living Things)

The phrase "Reverence for Life" was coined by Albert Schweitzer in 1915 when he was serving as a Missionary Medical Doctor in Lambarene, Gabon, West Africa. I'll seek to define the term before giving some background, but I've used it because I believe it encapsulates a necessary attitude to all living things and the total environment if we are to maximise wellbeing on planet earth.

"Reverence" is a term with definite religious connotations, meaning a suitable attitude towards deity of any description and to what is regarded as sacred. When Moses, the Jewish leader, prophet was approaching a vision of a burning bush he was told to take his shoes off because he was on holy ground. People in some religions remove their shoes as a sign of reverence when they are entering a structure used for worship. Years ago in Western society when men wore hats, they would remove them on entering a church as a sign of reverence. Schweitzer was suggesting that we adopt this attitude towards the whole of life.

Schweitzer was a brilliant individual. He had doctorates in Philosophy, Music and Theology before he decided he needed to train in a more practical field to more directly help those with great needs. He studied to be a medical doctor and offered for missionary work.

When he came up with the phrase "Reverence for Life" he had been called to tend a dying woman up river from his mission station. He was, at the time, working on another book "The Philosophy of Civilisation" and since the Western world was engaged in World War I he was seeking to come up with a course he could suggest to overcome this urge of human kind to kill one another. The boat he was travelling on in the late afternoon of the third day out was held up by a herd of hippopotamuses. He was at first very frustrated at the delay but the thought occurred to him that they were in their natural environment and he and his party were the intruders. He wrote "there flashed upon my mind, unforeseen and unsought, the phrase, "Reverence for Life". The iron door had yielded: the path in the thicket had become visible."[36] It is high time human kind adopted such an attitude.

Frederick Pohl in a book whose writing he shared with Isaac Asimov "Our Angry Earth" commented, "It is already too late to save our planet from harm. Too much has happened already: farms have turned into deserts, forests have been clear cut to wasteland, lakes have been poisoned, and the air is filled with harmful gases."[37]

Perhaps humankind getting itself in perspective would help towards adopting an attitude of reverence for life. In a brilliant article in the Weekend Australian Magazine of 19 January 19 2013, Philip Adams drew attention to the use of Auld Lang Syne on New Year's Eve since Robert Burns penned the lyrics. He suggests that singing the song to herald in 2013 doesn't involve sufficient "auldness". He wrote 2013 is not only an arbitrary figure but an awesome arithmetical error. 2013? How about adding 449,997,987 years to round it off at the official figure of 4.5 billion. That's how many New Years this planet has had since it opened for business - with a fireworks display somewhat

[36] "My Life and Thought" Albert Schweitzer p.141
[37] "Our Angry Earth", Isaac Asimov

larger than the few sparklers over Sydney Harbour. Yet we reduce that awesomeness, that immensity to four silly little numbers. We date history and New Years from the hypothetical birthday of a bloke called Jesus. [The Jewish and Hindu calendars take the figure into the 500ths - but it is still petty cash.] To focus all this attention on the past two millennia is like making a huge amount of fuss over the final sleeper on the Nullarbor railway line while ignoring the rest of the track or picking up a pebble by Cheop's tomb while dismissing his pyramid.

... billion New Years. Time enough for the great engines of geology and evolution to provide us with a particularly lustrous orb crowded with its menageries, aviaries and aquariums. Deep oceans, high mountains, veldts and valleys, every nook and cranny with its birds and beetles, flora, fauna and fish."

Later in the article he comments "Despite our best efforts to kill ourselves off - around 150 million dead in wars and genocides in the last century alone - we've out-bred the rabbits and cane toads to become somewhat pestilential."

An article in the Courier Mail of Monday 16 July 2007 by Michael Hanlon endorses Philip Adam's thought and suggests that this planet would do very well without us, indeed that the rest of life would rejoice to see the back of us. Michael Hanlon was reporting on a book by Alan Weisman of Arizona University "The World Without Us". He speaks of the effects of radiation on some forms of life, given that the most likely demise of the human race would come about from nuclear activity.

"Much to everyone's surprise the flora and fauna round the Chernobyl disaster site have thrived." If humankind for whatever reason disappears. "Quickly the oceans would cleanse themselves; and similarly, the air, the creeks and the rivers. In a remarkably short time, Mother Nature would reassert herself over her old dominions. +In this new people-free world, a few species would do badly - the rats, cockroaches and starlings that cling to our coat tails would suffer. So would cattle, sheep and other farm animals … most wild species would thrive. By 2100, the half a million surviving African elephants would have multiplied to their pre-colonial population of 10 million or so. Africa's plains and forests would quickly fill with the great menagerie of game that once foraged and migrated unhindered across the continent. The jungles would start to regrow."

The articles by Philip Adams and Michael Hanlon highlight the incredible arrogance of human beings which has led very often to the thought that everything that exists may be exploited for the benefit of humans. This arrogance has led to the confining of chickens to cages for the whole of their lives, when the species is meant to scratch in the earth and be free to move and meting out the same confinement to pigs.

Hopefully no such calamity as outlined by Michael Hanlon will befall humankind and our sometimes rather tenuous relationship with other forms of life will continue. To adopt the attitude of reverence for life means that we will respect other forms of life and the earth and not wilfully kill or destroy any part of it. I don't intend to list the dire effects humans have had on the earth and its creatures, enough to say that countless species have been made extinct and that air pollution has reached a stage in some areas in which at sometimes people are not able to tolerate being outdoors.

It needs to be said that Albert Schweitzer was not a vegetarian nor did he suggest the preservation of the breeding cycles of mosquitoes.

I believe that the contribution of reverence for life towards individual and group harmony is obvious. If one mistreats other forms of life it can be almost guaranteed that sooner or later the same lack of regard will be shown to other human beings. To be in harmony with the earth and its creatures is to be in harmony with all that has life.

I want to suggest that if your beliefs do not result in an attitude of "Reverence for Life", they are inadequate and need revision.

THE CHECKLIST IN REVIEW

The ten items in the checklist range from how we as human individuals view ourselves, to relationships with other human beings and with all that has life. They deal with attitudes which negatively affect harmony and those which positively promote it.

These ten items constitute what I consider to have the greatest bearing on harmonious living.

A reminder of the main thesis of this book that our beliefs govern the way we act and react and that the final value of our beliefs is indicated by the way we treat others, ourselves, all that has life and the earth.

Perhaps you could go through the checklist and see how your behaviour relates to it and ask yourself if you are happy with your responses. Then ask what part of your beliefs may need changing if you are not satisfied.

In the final section of this book there are a number of exercises designed to help towards discerning your ideas and attitudes and giving them close scrutiny.

Suggestions for the Most Effective Use of the Ideas in this Book

You may like to follow through this section with one or more others and so be able to discuss your responses.

The Preamble

Second Principle

That unless someone is in some way severely mentally impaired, they have beliefs.

Jot down your beliefs:-

i.   Maybe they are largely in accord with a formal creed or statement of belief. If that's the case ask yourself if you thoroughly agree with them, particularly if they contradict outcomes in the checklist.

ii. Maybe you haven't ever written down what you believe. It is a valuable exercise. Ask yourself what you believe about the following as a starter - human beings - yourself, other people, the earth, other forms of life, list what you regard as being most important and then rank order them - 1 beside the most important and so on.

THE CHECKLIST
AND YOU

1. Getting Oneself in Perspective

   Given that our survival instinct is primary - do you ever put the needs of others before your own, spouse or partner, or children?

   How far do your concerns extend beyond yourself and your family?

   Do you give yourself a chance to be aware of needs other than those of family and friends, through news of some description?

   Have you got beyond throwing some sort of tantrum if things don't go the way you want them?

   How much do you resist people impinging on your privacy?

   Go back to the excerpt from Alain de Botton's book and re read it. Compared to the total universe we are infinitesimal. This is a good exercise in times when we are rather full of ourselves. There may be other memories you have if the actual experience is not immediately possible, such as looking across a series of mountain ranges from a peak, or looking across a stretch of ocean.

2. Each Individual has a Vital and Unique Place

Jot down 5 of your strengths - don't stop the exercise until you have 5. It may take longer than one session. You may like to check with family and/friends.

What are your abilities and aptitudes? Note - you may never have won anything or may not be at the top of your field.

Have you accepted yourself and recognised you have a place in the world?

Do you accept the way you look and are you happy in your own skin?

Consider the following discussion questions - perhaps you could discuss them with others.

What can you tell about a person's self-esteem by the way she/he walks, talks, dresses, and makes choices?

Who helps to form your self-esteem?

How do people change the way they feel about themselves? How do you?

What do you think are the advantages of good self-esteem?

From your observation of prominent people (think of a few), what would you say about their level of self-esteem?

Is there anything wrong with having high self-esteem?

What are some of the things which can cause people to have low self-esteem?

Why do you think that some people have problems thinking about their good points?

Is it possible for a brilliant, attractive, sporty person to have a low self-esteem? Why?

Why is jealousy a symptom of low self-esteem?

What is modesty?

Why are failures an important part of life?

What can you do if there is something you really dislike about yourself (e.g. a big nose)?

Imagine you are the leader of a group starting a new course or project and you want to inspire the confidence of the members. Devise a "pep talk".

Make a list of 20 words that describe people positively e.g. understanding, compassionate, energetic, optimistic.

Make a list of character traits that you hope people see in you.

Turn each of these negative attitudes into positives - reckless, passive, uninformed, irresponsible, disorganised, untrustworthy, listless, impatient, directionless, unfocussed, and unmotivated.

List 5 people who show care toward you.

Give examples of how you co-operate with people you live or work or enjoy leisure activities with.

How have you shown your honesty this week?

Describe one way you show respect for yourself?

Describe one way you show respect for another person?

Give an example of a time it took courage for you to do something.

List things you are responsible for.

Describe a time when you learned to do something difficult because you kept on trying.

3. A Sense of Community

    Draw 5 concentric circles. This can be roughly done. In the centre one write ME. Then in the other circles from inside out write, Family, close friends; Acquaintances, Community; Nation, Culture; The Earth. Now go back and jot down what each of these contribute to us as individuals. (one for "the earth"- other animals. The point of the exercise is to help us realise that we are never really alone.

4. A Minimising of Tribalism

    Make two columns. Head one US and the other THEM. Now make two lists of people you would put under each heading.

    What is the first thing which comes into your mind when you consider the following list - boat people, aboriginal, gay person, European, American, someone from UK, someone from a rival state, bikie.

    Do you consider your reactions stereotypes?

    Tribalism is minimised when we actually meet people we stereotype. Wherever possible take the opportunity to meet groups you may be unfamiliar with.

5. <u>Tolerance, Openness, Forgiveness</u>

How tolerant are you? How do you rate yourself on a scale of 1-10 with 1 being prepared to listen to opposing views and 10 being militantly settled in one's view point?

How true do you consider the following statements? These make great topics for discussion.

Violence and hate are never solutions to anger.

Groups of people should not be judged by the actions of a few.

All people deserve to be treated with fairness, respect and dignity.

Vengeance and justice are not necessarily the same.

History tells us that intolerance only causes harm.

Tolerance is a lifelong endeavour.

To be done

Model tolerance and compassion.

Avoid stereotyping people or countries.

Read books that address prejudice, tolerance and hate.

Undertake projects to help those in need with people from diverse backgrounds.

Are you obsessed with getting revenge for some slight? How much room does this give you to get on with the rest of your life?

6. Sense of Humour

Are you a glass half full or a glass half empty person? If the first applies, are you likely to gloss over some problematic situations? If the second applies, can you work at seeing positive possibilities when confronted with disappointments or with a problem?

If in doubt as to which applies ask the following questions:-

Do I get discouraged easily?

Do I get depressed more than I want to?

Do I fail more than I think I should?

What makes you laugh out loud? If you don't know, listen to yourself for the next few days and make a list of what makes you laugh.

Build yourself a collection of videos, books, cartoons, sounds, images, letters that make you smile or laugh. Can you imagine how these might aid your physical, mental or spiritual healing.

7. A Recognition of the Equality of the Sexes

Following are a list of personal qualities:-

Ambition, courage, gentleness, humility, integrity, poise, serenity, thoughtfulness, wisdom, beauty, curiosity, good body, humour, intelligence, purity, sex appeal, unselfishness, wit, charm, determination, graciousness, independence, loyalty, self-control, sincerity, warmth, common sense, flexibility, honesty, innocence, manners, sensitivity, strength, will power.

From the list above, choose the ten that you think are most important for a man to have and on a separate sheet and the ten you think is most important for a woman to have.

In each case put them in order so that the one you think is most important is at the top of the list and the least important at the bottom. If there are qualities which you think are important that are not included then put them in yourself.

Now compare your lists. Are there any similarities? Are there any differences? Could you make up one list which would apply to both? Which ones would be left out? Have a careful look at them. Is there any difference between them and the ones in your list?[38]

Sheryl Sandberg, Chief Executive Officer of Facebook has commented "The sisters are doing some of it to themselves. For a variety of reasons they're not aiming high enough. They're underestimating their abilities. They're doing too much housework and childcare. They're compromising their career goals for partners and children - even when such partners and children don't exist. 'We hold ourselves back in ways both big and small, by lacking self-confidence, by not raising our hands, and by pulling back when we should be leaning in.'"[39]

From your own perspective, what's your opinion on that statement? Rate your opinion on a scale of 1 to 10 with 1 being strongly agree and 10 being strongly disagree.

How do you regard people of the opposite sex? Read through the following list putting a tick beside the statements you agree with.

1. Pure sex object.
2. Not deserving of respect.
3. Need to keep their place.

---

[38] "Me, You and Others", Elizabeth Callister, Noel Davis, Barbara Pope
[39] Time Magazine article, 18 March 2013, "Confidence Woman", Belinda Luscombe

4. Capable of valid opinions.
5. Capable of being good companions.
6. Have a necessary role in society.

Are you happy with your opinion? What would have to happen to make you change your opinion?

8. <u>Accepting Varying Sexual Preferences</u>

How happy are you with your own sexual preference? Put a cross on the following scale indicating your preference.

_____

Very happy   Most unhappy

Where would you rate your attitude to homosexual or lesbian people?

_____

Very accepting   See them as outcasts

What would have to happen to change your response on either scale?

Is there anything in your beliefs to prevent a change?

How would you react if your child told you they were homosexual, lesbian or transsexual?

a. Reject them;
b. Try to persuade them otherwise; or
c. Be accepting/

If you are heterosexual, given the proof that homosexuality is biological/genetic if you or your beliefs or both insist on rejection, would you consider yourself homophobic?

9. <u>An Overall Espousal of Non-Violence and a Spurning of Gratuitous Violence</u>

Please work through the following questions.

How prone to violence are you?

Rate it on a scale of 1 to 10 with 1 being very slow and 10 being immediate reaction. Note violence may not involve a physical reaction, it could be verbal.

If you get very drunk, are you likely to become very violent? This could be an indication of your natural reaction to opposition but your inhibitions are lowered. Do you just give in to the demands of others with no attempt to argue even though you are not happy with the situation? If you have answered yes, are you happy with the way you are?

In outlining this part in the "checklist" mention was made of "Assertiveness" falling between aggression and submission. Following is a reinforcement of the idea.

Being assertive means:
• asking for what you want;

- without feeling guilty;
- without putting others down; and
- making sure that you are not taking away the rights of others.

Being submissive means:
- hoping others know what you want without telling them;
- feeling hurt and not telling anyone; and
- not standing up for yourself.

Being aggressive means:
- demanding what you want;
- not worrying if you hurt other people; and
- not respecting or considering other people's rights.[44]

Work out an assertive, a submissive and an aggressive response to the following situation. This exercise would probably be most usefully done in a discussion group of some sort.

You have arranged to have dinner with your partner in quite a long relationship. They are not at the restaurant at the arranged time when you get there. They eventually arrive 20 minutes late and this is the third time this has happened.

10. Reverence for Life

Re-read the pages of the book dealing with "Reverence for Life". Where do you place yourself on the scale below?

The Jains a sect of the Hindus sweep paths before they walk so they don't kill any form of life	Other forms of life and the earth need to dance to our tune

Answer the following questions - perhaps discuss them with family/and or friends. Is it ever right to resort to violence?

If a person has reverence for life should they be vegetarian?

Is it possible to ensure that people grow up with the attitude? How?

What bearing does this attitude have on capital punishment?

Do you think that watching violent movies, TV programs or video games has any effect on the development of reverence for life?

If someone adopted the attitude of "reverence for life" what would be their action and/or attitude towards the following?

1. Seeing an ant or other insect at one's feet when walking outside.

2. Coming across a spider in an inside corner of your house.

3. Coming across a snake basking in the sun on a track.

4. Seeing sundry pieces of rubbish during a regular walk.

5. Seeing a group of children mistreating another child, a dog, or some other animal.

6. Efforts to reduce emissions which affect the environment such as the carbon tax.

7. Opportunities to support organisations such as RSPCA, World Wildlife Fund.

8. Live animal exports, mulesing sheep.

9. Organisations such as Amnesty International, Red Cross, Medicines San Frontiers.

IN CONCLUSION – AN IMPASSIONED APPEAL

This appeal is to all who may read this book of whatever belief. It is to all, for you all have beliefs. The appeal is for you to ask the question, what positive good are they? Are you and your beliefs having a positive effect, first of all on your life and then like the rippling effect of a stone in a pond going out to family, friends, community and beyond to the world at large.

There are a number of you whose beliefs will include an end time. In such beliefs there is an urgency about engaging in positive action. Scientists also speak of a constant deterioration, but they often speak in millennia. No-one really knows if positive action is imperative because of some catastrophic ending to our planet but certainly no matter how old you are mortality suggests you have limited time to make a difference. My appeal is for you to check your beliefs, the starting point for change and how their effects measure up against the "checklist".

As people of goodwill from within and between our beliefs let us work for positive change.

BIBLIOGRAPHY

Armstrong, Karen. Twelve Steps to a Compassionate Life. London: Bodley Head 2011.

Asimov, Isaac and Frederick Pohl. Our Angry Earth. New York: Tor, A Tom Doherty Associates Book. 1991

Benson, Herbert. MD with Margaret Stark. Timeless Healing. Hodder and Stoughten 1996

Bodycomb, John. No Fixed Address. Spectrum Publications 2010

Callister, Elizabeth, Davis, Noel, Pope Barbara. Me You and Others. Brooks
Waterloo Publishers 1988

Davis, Noel, Pope, Barbara Not Just Me. The Jacranda Press 1993

_____ Me, You and Others (2) The Jacaranda Press 1990

De Botton, Alain. Religion for Atheists. Penguin Books 2012

Edser, Dr. Stuart. Being Gay, Being Christian, You Can Be Both. Exile Publishing 2012

Frankl, Victor E., Man's Search for Meaning. Washington Square Press 1963

_____. The Unheard Cry for Meaning. Hodder and Stoughton 1978

Harris, Thomas A.,MD I'm OK – Your'e OK. Random House Limited 1973

Howe, Reuel L. The Miracle of Dialogue New York: Seabury Press 1963

Kung, Hans and Kuschel, Karl-Josef. A Global Ethic. SCM Press 1993

Parkinson, Lorraine. The World Acording to Jesus. Spectrum Publications 2011

Pease, Allan & Barbara Why Men Don't Listen & Women Can't Read Maps. Pease

Training International 1998

Powell, John SJ Fully Human, Fully Alive. Tabor Publishing 1976

Pui-Lan, Kwok Globalization, Gender and Peace Building. Paulist Press 2012

Seligman, Martin. Learned Optimism. Alfred F. Knopf 1991

Schweitzer, Albert My Life and Thought. Guild Books 1931
_____. Reverence for Life The Pilgrim Press 1969

Sparks, Rev.Susan, Laugh Your Way to Grace. Skylight Paths 2012

ACKNOWLEDGMENTS

Computer assistance and Formatting – Wayne and Mary Anne Hill.

Cover Design Scott Thompson

Preliminary consultation Rev.Graeme Adsett, John Honeywill, Rev.John Mavor

Proof reading and general support – my wife Mary

ABOUT THE AUTHOR

Noel Davis BA, MDiv., ThD., Dip. Div., Dip. Ed. is a Uniting Church minister. He grew up in Graceville, Brisbane. He was educated at Graceville State School, Central Practising School and Brisbane Boy's College. He trained for the Methodist ministry at King's College, University of Queensland.

In 1959 he married Mary Morris. They have three children Paul, Stephen and Mark. After serving a Methodist Circuit in Oakey for 5 years the family moved to Fiji working in the Fijian Methodist Church. Mark contracted meningitis and was left with two thirds brain damage. After three years in Fiji the family moved to the USA seeking treatment for Mark. Noel served a United Methodist Church in San Diego for three years. The family moved to Denver, Colorado where Noel did more study at Iliff School of Theology for five years.

On return to Australia the family settled in Frankston, Victoria where Noel served as School Chaplain at Frankston High School for ten years. The family then moved back to Brisbane where Noel worked in the Personal Development Programme of the Queensland Education Department for two years. He then spent the last 11 years of his ministry as the Chaplain at Somerville House, a High School for girls.

Noel has collaborated in the writing of three books in the area of Human Relationships Education. He has also written a book on the life and work of his grandfather, Walter Taylor, a prominent builder, notably of a bridge across the Brisbane River.

Printed in the United States
By Bookmasters